C000101696

All is One

The Beginners Guide
to Pythagorean Numerology

by Aditi Ghosh

kindle direct publishing

I am thankful to my parents for having introduced me to life.

I am thankful to my husband for having introduced me to my life lessons.

I am thankful to my son for having introduced me to my life purpose.

CONTENTS

* THE CANONICAL RGB's

P

25   I (d)
26-28(d) I   x 3 (d)
29-31(d). 2   x 3
31-34   3   x 3
3?-3?   4   x 2 3/4
3?-40   5   x 2 1/2
40-43   6   x 2 3/4
43-46   7   x 3 (d)
46-50   8   x 3 1/2
50-53   9   x 3 (d)

PREFACE

Another Day in Paradise

In the vastness of the universe, I'm but a tiny speck of dust, trying to bring some light in people's lives. However tiny I maybe, inside me, lay millions of tales of galaxies. My lifetime perhaps is very small with respect to the stars outside, but when I look inside, it feels all is timeless.

My introduction to Numerology happened at a point when nothing was going right in my life and I was failing to understand why. I was sure I was right and I was giving my best, yet it felt like fighting a strong current from the opposite direction. Till date, this remains as one of the most painful memories of my life. I didn't realize then, but I was chasing unrealistic goals, trying to follow someone else's footsteps, hoping to land up at the same place as they did. I had accidentally started a venture with a faulty model and soon it had started to collapse. I particularly remember the time when I realized that my establishment won't last a day longer. All my resources were spent and I ended up having huge debts in the market which I was unable to pay back. It was then that I decided to stop and think.

Every day we get a new chance to restart our lives and every hour brings a new promise. The sun shines again after the darkest hour, so hope must never die. I woke up the next morning and decided to reflect back and see where I went wrong and what I could do next. This is when Numerology came into my life. Maybe when nothing works, this mystical science could show some direction.

Numerology made me realize however much I try, I would never become someone else and never have the same trajectory of experiences that someone else had. I am me and my story will be my alone. It is with Numerology that I could view my life from a different vantage point and change my perspectives. My chase ended when I realized all what I was looking for, was right around and I was so blinded that I just couldn't see it. Slowly my life started improving, my relationships started making more sense and I started recovering from the debts. Today I am financially stable and it's been a decade that I'm free of debts. I feel blessed having been able to help many others too through my gift of reading numbers.

This book aims at introducing you to this great science of Numerology connecting you to some of the most basic patterns of your blue-print through which you will be able to expand your awareness and face your inner conflicts with confidence. You would no more need to see your life as a jigsaw puzzle as all the missing pieces are about to fall in place. I wish you happy reading.

The Drowning Scorpion

Once upon a time, there lived a saint by the river side. Every morning he'd go to the river to bathe. One day while bathing, he spotted a little scorpion struggling in the water, trying to save itself from drowning. It was fighting for a single breath. He immediately knew that the scorpion won't survive as scorpions are not swimmers. So, it was for him to choose whether he would rescue it, or allow it to die. He decided to save and carefully picked it up and went on to set it on dry land. But before he could do so, the scorpion stung him.

The sharp burning sensation from the scorpion's sting numbed his finger and this made him instinctively flung his hand and the scorpion went flying back into the water. But, the saint soon gained back his composure and went back trying to rescue the troubled scorpion again. But, once again like before, the scorpion stung him before he could safely keep it on land. The saint was now in deep pain but he decided to try again.

One of the saint's disciples spotted the event. Seeing the saint in pain and agony, the disciple was outraged. He strongly requested him to leave the scorpion alone. He said, "That creature deserves to die. Why are you even trying to save it? Leave it in the water to drown!"

But, the saint ignored this request and refused to give up. He continued with his efforts and finally succeeded in saving the scorpion, while he himself ended up being seriously wounded. The disciple then carried the staggering saint to his hut, treated him for his wounds and waited for him to regain his consciousness.

After the saint recollected himself, his disciple asked, "How can you still smile? How foolish you were trying to save the scorpion! It nearly killed you!" The saint replied, "My dear child, there is no reason for bitterness. The scorpion did not sting me out of some evil intension neither did I save it going out of my way. It was his dharma (nature) to sting. Just as it is my dharma to save life. He was following his dharma and I was following mine."

~ Anonymous

You see, we try to make our lives complicated, but in reality life is very simple. It is just a matter of one kind of energy interacting with another. And the moment we are able to see ourselves for what kind of energy we are, and see others for what they are, the equation becomes very predictable. We start seeing the random fall into a pattern. So, the stinging scorpion couldn't shock the saint on an emotional level because he understood himself and understood who the scorpion was.

In our lives, we may encounter many people like this who may hurt us intentionally or unintentionally. But, we should not resent their actions thinking that they were out to get us. What they do, shouldn't affect our purpose. What they think shouldn't create limitations for us. We must continue to do what we believe in anyway because we are born for it. We must follow our path. We cannot expect everyone else to understand our journey because they are not meant to walk our path or be us anyway. Their ability to understand us will depend on their level of evolution. If they are as evolved as the saint, they'd simply know who we are. If they are like the scorpion, they may keep stinging.

As you read this book, you will be on a journey of discovering a clear method of understanding any person's character. You can have a look inside yourself, as well as any other person around you by just using two most basic details; one of them is the date of birth, while the other is the name. These are the two frequencies which each one of us was endowed with by the universe at birth. These can be simplified into five Primary Numbers and by studying these numbers we can gain more clarity on each person's life issues. The more you'd start gaining clarity on the meanings of numbers, the easier it will become for you so steer around the challenges in your life while at the same time supporting and guiding others who would seem to be facing issues with theirs. It doesn't matter how long you had been holding misconceptions about life, right now is the perfect time to start and change them. Let this moment begin a new process for you...

Look Inside and Awaken...

According to a Buddhist legend, once when Buddha was wandering around the countryside, shortly after his enlightenment, he encountered several villagers who thought he was an extraordinary man. They asked him, "Are you God?" "No," he replied. "Are you a magician?" "No," he replied. "Then who are you?" they asked. Buddha simply said, "I am awake." The word "Buddha" means "the awakened one"; the one who has attained eternal wisdom.

Many of us have a misconception regarding what we really are. The society has created a stereotype for each person. It is a general expectation that each person should be able to fit into a specific group or category so that the function of the society as a whole becomes easier. This is how herds are created. This is how even the lab rats are trained. To set our moral values, ever since our childhood, certain behaviors are rewarded and for others, we are punished repeatedly. We are being trained to fit in by responding in approved ways. Being thin and fair is considered to be more beautiful than being dark and stout, whereas the reality is, all colors are equally beautiful. Red, white, green, blue, black, all are equally appealing. Whether you are thin or you are curvy, what matters more is you should be fit and free from disease.

Your body can have any shape and color and you can still be beautiful.

When a child starts attending school, he realizes that if he has a question to ask, he has to raise his hand rather than interrupting the teacher. If he doesn't do so, the deviation from the accepted norm, would be considered abnormal. So, for the child, behaving in the typical manner is absolutely important because anything different, won't be accepted. So, generation after generation, we keep on inheriting the customs and ideologies practiced by our ancestors. We don't question why we should do it because if we question, we deviate and deviation from the herd means we are abnormal. But, we want to be perfectly normal and typical. So, we push ourselves to study long hours, obey authority, conform to all norms and then find a job suited to ensure future security. We teach ourselves day and night to be loyal employees. "I" must never ask for myself and just go on because in the end it will surely payoff to me. But does it?

If "I" am more aware, this perspective of fitting into a stereotype is most likely to change. "I" will realize how special "I" am. "I" am being born with unique set of talents of its own which no one else has. "I" am not abnormal, but really gifted. "I" don't need to be typical because "I" am irreplaceable. "I" am imperfect, yet "I" am complete and "I" am enough.

In this book,
I have decided to introduce you to "I"

When you say, "I understand", "I exist", "I imagine", who is this "I" exactly? After all, it is "I" who thinks and feels. It is "I" who doesn't change even when our thoughts, imaginations, desires and feelings change. In the process of becoming a butterfly, the caterpillar sheds its entire body several times, yet, its "I" remains the same. So, who is "I" and how can we look inside and find it?

The beauty of Numerology is,
it simplifies the chaos
and makes all of it fall in a pattern.

Looking inside becomes very simple when you break yourself down into some simple number codes. The five most important number codes that we are born with are called the Five Primary Numbers. These numbers create our Personality Chart. This chart reflects the qualities of our mind; the strengths and the weaknesses that are intrinsic to us. This is the domain over which we can have complete control. Our strengths are the things we can leverage on, something that comes easily to us. While our weaknesses may hold us back from achieving many great things. So, in order to have complete personal growth, we need to continuously remind ourselves to work upon them. But first, we need to identify them. We need to precisely realize the qualities that make us unique as this will help us understand how exactly to function. For instance, if we are looking at career options, we would be able to narrow down specific opportunities based on the things we know we are good at. We can also refrain from choosing options that may bring our weaknesses into focus. As a matter of fact, it is always better to focus more on our strengths instead of bringing our weaknesses into the limelight. By choosing to enhance our strengths, we will be able to get the best out of opportunities and keep away from falling into problems. Our overall performance in life will be upgraded.

The meanings of the five Primary Numbers which are the core components of our Personality Chart or the domain of our influence are explained below:

In this section I'd only explain the significance of these numbers. To know how to derive these numbers refer to the next section.

1. *The Life Path Number:*

Well, maybe you are in a hurry to reach your destination, but Numerology says life is a journey and it is the journey that matters more and not reaching the destination anyhow. So, first of all relax and try to enjoy the moment right now because this moment is your life. This one moment in brief describes how you will travel the whole path because how you do one thing shows how you do everything.

The Life Path Number is the most important component of your Personality Chart.

You could be aware of the path which you must follow or sometimes even be unaware of it. In either case if you just find out the meaning of this number code, you will simply know what to do and how to get cosmic support. The major confusion in your life will end.

It is important that you allow this number to play fully in your life. There can be situations which may make you sway from your path because life will never be without challenges and the realization of your Life Path or Life Lesson may not come easy to you. Yet, the cosmic forces will ensure you are being pushed towards it anyways. Remember challenges are nothing, but lessons in your path which will help you in strengthening your character. Through these challenges, you will learn to improve upon your weaknesses and develop your strengths. So, embrace your path and the challenges that come along.

2. *The Destiny Number:*

This is the second-most important number for you to take note of. The previous number, the Life Path or the Life Lesson number, as I mentioned describes the path which you are supposed to follow and the lessons which you are supposed to learn in this lifetime. The Destiny number on the other hand indicates the goals which you are supposed to achieve by following your Life Path. Once again, it is important to note that no one; neither you nor anyone else would be able to reach your goals too easy without even fighting for it.

Challenges actually will make life interesting
And overcoming them,
Will make life meaningful...

Unlike the Life Path number, the Destiny number is always present in your awareness, unless your birth name was changed at an early age. If your Birth Name was modified, it will strongly subdue the effect of the original Destiny number, but not completely diminish it. To learn more about the effect of Modified Names, refer to **Chapter 8**.

The Destiny Number is derived from your first full name after birth and the influence of this number always remains even if you change your name. So, realize that there is no running away from it. However you can add certain missing qualities in your character with the help of a name change and smooth your journey towards your destiny.

The Destiny Number represents a target that you chase every day. It reveals certain talents and abilities that you were born with; the degree of evolution of your soul when you were born and the information contained within that. This number represents ultimately where you will end up.

All this melodrama for what when ultimately you're going to be back to square one! What then remains to be done? Well, a lot.

***Each number defines
a wide spectrum of possibilities
and the more you get acquainted
with a number,
more possibilities
you will be able to discover.***

*In this life through which you will travel,
there will be endless discoveries.
So, remain open because even when you know,
you exactly don't know what will be coming.*

3. <u>***The Soul Number:***</u>

I consider this number to be the third most important number in our Numerology blue-print. This number indicates the information that you have collected over the previous lifetimes. Well, yes, I am indicating the philosophy of reincarnation out here and I really plan to elaborate further on the philosophy of reincarnation as it is very interesting, but maybe not in this book.

Now, coming back to this number; the information that you were exposed to during your previous lifetimes have shaped your deepest desires and dreams in the present lifetime. These desires could be so strong within you that they may totally suppress the effect of all other numbers in your blue-print. The Life Path and Destiny numbers may fall weaker if not your Soul number is in tune. This number will always play a strong role behind determining most of your choices in life.

The Life Path, Destiny and Soul, together indicate three most important dots in your blue-print which are absolutely necessary to connect. Mentioned next are the other two dots which will form a vital part of the qualities that you project outside.

4. *The Personality Number:*

This number indicates the aspects of your character that you reveal to the outside world. When this number matches with the Soul Number, it indicates you are a very genuine person. But, usually most of us are not so. In most cases you will see that the Personality number gives different information as compared to the Soul Number.

The Personality number reflects your mannerisms, body language and all the non-verbal signals of communication that you send out at the onset of any relationship. But, as people come closer and get to know you better, they slowly sense your true inner character.

5. _**The Birthday Number:**_

Amongst the five Primary Numbers, I am mentioning this number last because to me this is lesser important than the other four numbers which provide more clues to how the qualities of your brain could be. However, even then, your birthday is very important because it will mark the onset of every important life cycle in your life. This makes it a very important day of your life.

The Birthday number indicates certain key characteristics which are inherent to you. Also when you see this number with respect to your Life Path number, it reveals some more details about your journey of life.

**The five Primary Numbers play a key role in defining more-or-less who you are, what your purpose in life is and how you can be happy.**

Mentioned below are the methods by which you can derive each of these numbers for yourself.

Let us take an example as below:

Name – Prabir Chandra Paul
Date of Birth – 23rd January 1947

1. *The Life Path Number:*

This number is calculated from your date of birth. To calculate this number, you need to first reduce the year number (which is 1947 in this case) into a double-digit value (1 + 9 + 4 + 7 = 21). Then you have to add all the three double-digit values (the month of January would be a single-digit value) to find the final double-digit sum. The final step would be reducing the final double-digit value to get the single-digit base code. In Pythagorean Numerology, the thumb rule is to reduce all values to a final single-digit base code. You must always do it irrespective of whichever value you are dealing with. This final base code is considered to be most strongly expressed.

Now, let us see the calculation:

23rd January 1947
= 23 + 1 + (1 + 9 + 4 + 7)
= 23 + 1 + 21
= 45

= 4 + 5

= 9 (This would be written as Life Path 45/9)

As you can see, the Life Path number out here reduces to 45/9, in which 45 is the double-digit code and the final base value for the name is 9. So, 9 is the basic Life Path number out here and the code 45 derived before the final reduction, provides finer information about the base Life Path. There can be other ways too by which you could be deriving a 9 base code with different birth dates, for example, it could be 18/9 or 27/9 or even 63/9, and each double digit variation would have the same base quality, but the finer qualities would be different. For this reason each variation of 9 would tell a unique story of its own.

2. *The Destiny Number:*

This number is calculated from your first full name after birth. Please note that you have to use the full name (including the first, middle and last all of it). The example case has first, middle and last names. In case you don't have a middle name, only use the first and last names.

Over the years several people have also repeatedly asked me whether or not they must include the honorifics like Mr., Ms., Mrs., Dr., Sir, Lady, Sr., Jr., Captain, Father, Sister, etc. while calculating. Well, my answer is, No! Please only use the name!

To go about the calculation, first you need to know that each letter of the alphabet resonates to a particular number. You can find the chart below and see the numeric values of all the letters:

Pythagorean Alphabet Chart

1	2	3	4	5	6	7	8	9
A	B	C	D	E	F	G	H	I
J	K	L	M	N	O	P	Q	R
S	T	U	V	W	X	Y	Z	

Once you know the numeric values of all the letters, you have to arrange these numeric values with respect to the letters of your name, add the numbers, derive the sum and finally reduce it to a single digit base value by using the number reduction method. Once again, reducing to a single-digit base value is a thumb-rule.

```
7 9 1 2 9 9    3 8 1 5 4 9 1    7 1 3 3  = 82/1
P R A B I R    C H A N D R A    P A U L
```

As you can see, the name above reduces to 82/1, hence, the double-digit code 82 out here provides the finer information and 1 is the base information.

3. *The Soul Number:*

This number too is calculated from your first full name after birth. To calculate this, you have to short-list all the vowels in the name and then add the numeric values of the vowels derive the sum and finally reduce it to a single-digit base value.

$$
\begin{array}{ccccc}
1 \ 9 & & 1 & 1 & 1 \ 3 & = \ 16/7 \\
P\,R\,A\,B\,I\,R & C\,H\,A\,N\,D\,R\,A & & P\,A\,U\,L
\end{array}
$$

As you can see, the Soul Number out here reduces to 23/5. The vowels as we know are A, E, I, O and U but, in the above example, we only have A, E, I and O as vowels. *In some cases, the letters "Y" and "W" are also considered to be vowels. It happens when they play the role of a vowel in a speech sound or a syllable. For example, in the names "Surily", "Yves" or "Mary", "Y" plays the role of a vowel sound before or following a consonant. However, in the names "Yousef" or "Joyee", the "Y" is playing the role of a consonant followed by a vowel sound. Similarly in the names "William" or "Weston", "W" plays the role of a consonant. However, in the names "Dwight" or "Gwen", specifically where "W" follows the letters "D and "G", it is considered to be a vowel.*

4. *The Personality Number:*

This number, once again is calculated from your first full name post birth. It is the sum of numeric values of all the consonants in your name reduced to a single-digit base code.

```
7 9   2   9   3 8   5 4 9     7     3  = 66/3
P R A B I R   C H A N D R A   P A U L
```

We can see that the Personality Number out here is 66/3

5. *The Birthday Number:*

Deriving this number is simplest of all. It is basically your date of birth reduced to a single-digit. For example, Prabir Chandra Paul was born on the 23rd of January 1947. So, his Birthday Number would be 23/5.

Each of these numbers uncovers hidden meanings related to your life purpose. Each number represents an energy or frequency which can be allowed to play to its full potential. Each form of energy can be made to act either in its positive end or in its negative end. Energy is neither good nor bad and it all depends on how we use it and what we end up tapping. It is possible we could be unknowingly tapping the negative end of our energies and activating our weaknesses.

The five Primary Numbers are like dots waiting to be joined by you. Sooner or later all dots will join...

These numbers outline endless possibilities waiting to be realized. Once all the dots are connected, you will be able to make sense of every random life experience that you passed through. Nothing happened in your life without a reason. Even the worst of the experiences were actually wonderful strokes of luck which have brought you here finally. Things might not have turned up the way you wanted, but, you are exactly where you should have been.

3.   NUMBER VIBRATIONS

**"If you want to find the secrets of the universe,
Think in terms of energy, frequency and
vibrations."**

~ Nikola Tesla

Everything vibrates. A rock may look like one solid chunk, but within the solid rock there are millions and millions of subatomic particles tightly packed together. Although tightly packed, the molecules still vibrate. If this solid state of matter is subjected to heat, the heat may compete with the attraction between the molecules and can lead them to grow apart. This movement can then lead to change of the state of matter. Similarly, every other physical reality around us too can be broken down into the molecule level and at that level everything is vibrating and is prone to the change of states when some specific frequency of energy is applied to it. Everything moves and everything breaks; you just have to know the frequency at which it will.

The most potent form of energy is how we think.
Our thoughts are cosmic waves
penetrating all time space.

Our thoughts are free to go anywhere anytime. Where we send them, how we think, and how we act upon, creates who we are. Everything around us is just a matter of one kind of energy interacting with another; our personal energies are interacting with the energies of the people we encounter and also with the energies in our surroundings. When the two energies are compatible, the interaction is harmonious, while when two energies are incompatible, there is discord.

Energy in itself is neither good nor bad. It is just raw energy. It is neither wrong nor right. Basically, you cannot fit anything into these two categories. The idea of wrong and right will always be relative. Moral relativism says what I think to be wrong could only be wrong for me, but right for someone else.

Everything that you dislike in a person
could be perfectly likeable by someone else.

While learning the Pythagorean Theorem in school, little did I know that time would strengthen my association with his ideologies. I did not have the slightest idea about his spiritual and philosophical contributions back then. I was only amazed by the beauty of his theorem which superficially appeared to be applicable only for right angled triangles, but soon we realized that it was applicable for almost any closed shape.

I wouldn't have been interested in Numerology if not for the name Pythagoras which came to me for the second time when I coincidentally started delving into the subject. I was surprised that the same old name associated with the magic theorem, was also connected to Numerology. I wondered how it was even possible. I believed scientists and mathematicians have nothing to do with intuitionism after all. But, as I read about him, I learnt, he was much more than just being a mathematician. Mathematics to him was rather a spiritual experience.

"God built the Universe on Numbers."

~ Pythagoras

To us today his derivations may seem to be very obvious and simplistic, but at the time when he discovered them, a cult of mathematicians had started following and worshipping him like God. They felt, he had superpowers.

4.   THE CARDINAL NUMBERS

Once you start interpreting everything in terms of energy and learn the language of numbers, it's hard to free your brain from their tangle. They seem so very natural and innate; it feels like they are something that you are just born with. In this Chapter, I wish to discuss the mystical meanings associated with the single-digit numbers. These single-digit values are also called **Cardinal Numbers**.

Mentioned below you'd find the interpretation of all the Cardinal Numbers. It is important for you to note wherever the number appears, the basic meaning of the number doesn't change, only the interpretation changes as per the placement in your blueprint. And interpreting the number properly as per the placement and combination with other numbers is the most difficult part of Numerology. For this reason, I have placed the varying meanings of each Cardinal Number as per its possible placement in a blueprint so that it becomes easier for you to understand the mixed equation of numbers. In the end I have also mentioned the issues that each number may activate which one must pay attention to. It is important to keep in mind these negative aspects of each number because not knowing them may cause more damage than good.

1 **Basic Meaning:** This is the number of creation; the first primal force and the first raw energy. It is that one number from which all other numbers can be formed. It is the creator and the pioneer, striking out alone. This number makes a person independent and very individualistic. He is likely to play a strong force and lead a group. 1 also gives a strong sense of responsibility and the raw energy to accomplish any task. This number is highly competitive, decisive and courageous.

"If you can't fly then run,
If you can't run then walk,
If you can't walk then crawl,
But whatever you do
You have to keep moving forward."

~ Martin Luther King

Life Path 1: This is a path of independence and self-motivation. You are here to bring positive and creative energy into the world. So, you have to overcome your insecurities and express your creative energies to the fullest. You can do so by channelizing your beautiful energies into any field: writing, painting, designing, sculpture, business, sports, music or theatre. Your motive should just be bringing energy and innovation into this world.

There could be a non-stop inner voice within you, telling you that you are not good enough, but it is your challenge to overcome this inner voice of criticism and become emotionally stable, secure and self-dependent. You have to believe in yourself because you are born with raw power. It is only a matter of time that you realize this power within. You have to learn to make your own decisions and stand by them, regardless of whatever others may think of you. You must make sure that you are an original. You do not need to follow the crowd or need the support of others to make your decisions. No matter what, you can take the road less travelled.

Destiny Number 1: If your Destiny number is 1, you are destined to be the leader in your field. You have a lot of energy and you are best at initiating things. You are destined to be the in-charge and will never be happy playing the second-lead. You like to be in the limelight. You must know that your goal is to continuously develop your own individuality and bring out your uniqueness. However, be careful of not carrying this out to extreme levels of selfishness.

Soul Number 1: When 1 comes as your Soul number, you surely like to be the best at whatever you do. You desire to be the leader; respected and appreciated by all. Winning competitions gives you thrills and plays the main motive behind most of your actions. You may project something else outwardly, but if your Soul is 1, there is bound to be this competitive streak strongly there in you.

Personality Number 1: When 1 comes up as your Personality number, you project an image of being independent, responsible, enthusiastic and individualistic. You project a very strong personality and appear active, powerful, competitive, focused and efficient. Your high level of creativity also gets noticed by people.

Birthday Number 1: If your Birthday number is 1, it gives you qualities of strong individuality, high energy levels coupled with good amount of creative and leadership abilities. You also have great ambition and a very strong drive for success. You are original, creative and innovative and you can motivate others and bring out their best.

Issues with 1: This is a number strongly connected to creativity, originality, innovation and self-dependence. When used positively, these energies can change the world in a better way. When used negatively, these can also destroy the world. It is true that this number creates a leader in the true sense, but, many a times such people also become leaders of terror camps and criminal activities and follow these negative goals with strong determination.

The negative side of this number can set people on a headstrong path, where they don't really care even if their actions cause dire consequences for others. It is also seen that people with this number find it very difficult to form partnerships. They could often be seen making sudden impulsive decisions without the consent of others.

Determination is a very strong quality, but, it is also important to balance it with wisdom and tact. It has to be seen that the strong drive to find individuality doesn't turn into extreme selfishness.

2 *Basic Meaning:* This number plays the mediator trying to balance the two opposite poles and brings harmony. It represents love, cooperation and partnerships. This number is passive, tactful and patient. It is happy to stay in the background acting as the power behind the throne, rather than coming into the limelight. It has no problems with following the authority and wants to fit in. It sacrifices and compromises, yet also feels the need to be appreciated for its efforts. It is always socially aware of others, tries to gather ideas through other people and seeks their approval. It is kind, soft, emotional and accepting.

> *"I can do things that you cannot,*
> *You can do things I cannot;*
> *Together we can do great things."*

> ~ *Mother Teresa*

Life Path 2: This is a path of learning to be cooperative and supportive and to be able to work in coordination with others by avoiding conflicts. You have to learn to do the balancing act; by balancing the interests of both sides or by balancing your own needs versus the need of others. It is okay to compromise and subordinate your own needs sometimes, but not always. You must make a firm point by using discretion. Your path is about finding love and harmony and about bringing people together. You will do best when you will play the mediator of some kind by connecting two people or two entities.

You could be socially and emotionally aware of people and can acutely feel what others could be experiencing. Through these experiences of their agonies, you can feel their inner turmoil. You feel empathy and always try to help and support. But remember to never become too involved and entangled in their lives because if you do so, you may end up becoming a part of the problem.

Destiny Number 2: When your Destiny number is 2, you are destined to bring people together. You must remember to never play a role in separating them as then you will be acting against your purpose. You are supposed to connect people and promote peace and harmony between them. You can also act as an ambassador between two bodies and contribute in creating tactful and diplomatic relationships. You must find the middle path and always avoid conflicts and confrontations.

Soul Number 2: If your Soul number is 2, you are very conscious of what other people think about you. You want to fit in and so, you always try to find the middle-path and make others feel happy. You are warm, soft and cooperative and you do not want to become a part of any controversy or confrontation. You do not crave limelight; rather feel happier by playing the mind behind the person in the forefront. However, if you are hurt, you do not stop being political and manipulative behind the scenes.

Personality Number 2: If your Personality number is 2, you project a soft, cooperative, loving, unthreatening and friendly image of yours to the outside world. You appear to be very patient, kind, accepting and empathetic. You are always ready to listen and people find it easy to open up to you. This is why you become popular among your friends.

Birthday Number 2: When 2 comes up as your Birthday number, it gives you tactful and diplomatic qualities. With this, you are friendly and cooperative and are able to work well in partnerships. You are good with keeping people together. You can be highly emotional and also have distinct intuitive abilities. You are aware of your surroundings and easily get influenced by the emotional ambience around you.

Issues with 2: Sometimes this number makes a person so much supportive and helpful that they may completely overlook their own needs and end up doing what someone else thinks they should. The 2s have troubles saying "No" to others and draw their boundaries. They feel too vulnerable to what others may demand from them, feeling totally confused about where to draw the line. They end up doing too much and when their efforts are not reciprocated, they suddenly withdraw support all at once and rock the boat violently.

It is important for them to realize that 2 stands for balance and achieving balance is extremely necessary for them. There should be a balance between give and get. There should be a balance between what they desire and what others expect from them.

3 **Basic Meaning:** This is the number of emotional sensitivity, optimism, creativity and self-expression. This number gives an extremely strong drive for creativity and expression of ideas. This is the number of a performer. It indicates a person who loves to enjoy life to the fullest and is filled with optimism. With a 3, a person must develop his skill with words and cultivate the art of conversation.

> *"I always think a great speaker*
> *convinces us not by force of reasoning,*
> *but because he is visibly enjoying*
> *the beliefs he wants us to accept."*
>
> ~ *William Butler Yeats*

Life Path 3: If your Life Path is 3, your expressive drive is very powerful however, you may not be completely aware of the power with words which you can develop. It is important for you to realize and cultivate upon it. You should find various ways of creatively expressing yourself and never block your true emotional expression. You must know that you have strong emotions and this is your gift. You have to use this emotional sensitivity to bring positive message to the world.

There is an innate tendency within you towards giving advice to people. You have to know that the best way for you to succeed in life is to act on the same advice that you give out to others. You can be a great speaker if you cultivate upon it and that will generate many followers for you too. You will show strong talents in making other people believe in your ideas.

It is important to note that you will never do well if you choose a job which makes you spend long hours in confinement. It is your need to be involved in many experiences and enjoy life.

Destiny Number 3: If your Destiny number is 3, your destiny then is to motivate people. You are extremely creative and are destined towards being in the field of performing arts, writing or even motivational speaking. You would strive to make people's lives better and more colorful; hence you can also be a great artist, stylist or a designer. You will have multiple talents, but, you must focus your energies in one direction and solidify your skills in that. You must keep yourself from squandering away your beautiful talents.

Soul Number 3: If you have 3 as a Soul number, it means you seek happiness and find it in making others happy. You love to express your ideas through words and other forms of expression. Unhappy people make you unhappy too, so you try to uplift people wherever you go. You bring the message of hope and courage to the world. You also are very emotional and romantic and being in love is very important to you.

Personality Number 3: If your Personality number is 3, you project a very upbeat personality. Your appearance is very important to you and so, you love to dress up and look well-groomed. Strong communication skills are also a very important part of your personality.

Birthday Number 3: When you have 3 as your Birthday number, it gives you creative abilities and a way with words. You appear to be joyous and optimistic and are a great communicator. You also have high imaginative and creative abilities. People feel uplifted in your company and seek your advice.

Issues with 3: This is the number of expression, yet interestingly, many people with strong 3s in their Numerology charts find it difficult to express their true emotions either because they are too shy, or because they fear criticism and rejection. They may feel a need to be perfect and end up repressing their emotional vulnerability. But, unless true emotions are expressed and vulnerability shown, there is no connection. Without a connection, everything feels superficial.

A 3 person needs to understand that showing true emotions would make him appear authentic and believable. Criticism shouldn't be seen as a form of rejection, but as a clue to improve upon the pitch a bit further.

It is seen that many 3s may even have a pessimistic outlook towards life. Forget optimism, they could be only seeing dark clouds all the time and could be manic depressives. It is only when they focus on their true talents that they discover their power.

4 **Basic Meaning:** This number represents firmness, security, stability, reason, logic and method. This is a number of all earthly, solid and tangible things. It represents a builder. This would indicate an honest, solid and stable person who would tirelessly work towards creating future security. This would be a steady worker depending on whom enterprises can be built.

> *"Our goals can only be reached*
> *through a vehicle of a plan,*
> *in which we must fervently believe,*
> *and upon which we must vigorously act.*
> *There is no other route to success."*

> *~ Pablo Picasso*

Life Path 4: If 4 comes up as your Life Path number, it means that you are on a path towards achieving security and stability by slowly following a step-by-step process. Your purpose in life is to be able to build a solid foundation on which you and others can rely. You have to follow the path of seeing logical and visible results through your efforts. If something doesn't seem to be logical, it surely is not for you. You will be more equipped in dealing with tangible reality, business and finances. You have to always make your judgments based on reason and common sense. You have to see that you always deal in practical objects through which people can benefit.

You would also show a natural ability towards fixing and managing machines and solving tiresome puzzles. You are always open towards acquiring more knowledge in your field of interest. You have an overactive mind which never ceases to work; hence, you must look for positive outlets to keep your mind engaged.

Destiny Number 4: If your Destiny number is 4, you are destined to become exceptionally skilled in your chosen field. You will show attention to details and great depth of knowledge in your subject and will be able to build something tangible and substantial through which people can benefit. You would love to learn and teach your learning. You will be good with handling finances and will show a business-minded attitude.

Soul Number 4: If 4 comes up as your Soul number, it means you are a very methodical, grounded, practical and organized person. You feel fulfilled when you know that you have been able to secure your future. You are loyal, level-headed and dependable and you believe in square deals. This number gives a business-minded outlook to a person. It is always seen that a 4 person is good with handling finances cautiously.

Personality Number 4: If 4 comes up as your Personality number, you present a dependable, level-headed and reliable picture of yours to the outside world. You appear cautious, efficient and logical. You present a work-oriented and industrious attitude to people.

Birthday Number 4: When your Birthday number is 4, you tend to be very orderly and methodical. You have great attention to details and are very hard-working. However, you can be very blunt with your words and once you choose to argue, you won't give up your ground easily. You would produce solid evidence to prove your point. _

Issues with 4: This is a number of stability and security and often it is seen that people with strong 4s in their blue-prints are seen to be struggling with issues related to the same in their early lives. Many of them face early life family issues and end up growing up in the lack of a stable or secure foundation. It is the test of time through which they learn the importance of what a solid foundation means.

Many 4s are also prone to over processing and overanalyzing the situation while making decisions. This results in confusion and they often get caught up in mental loops. It is during this time that they need some moral support and encouragement otherwise they may end up making impulsive decisions. They also find it difficult to deal with change and try to resist it for as long as they can.

5 **Basic Meaning:** This number seeks change, adventure and freedom. It is flexible, adaptable, versatile and curious. It has a free-wheeling energy and wants to experience variety of things. With this a person is seen to be highly free-spirited. Someone, who wishes to go out in his pursuit of curiosity, this person cannot be controlled, confined or fenced.

> *"Since life is short and the world is wide,*
> *the sooner you start exploring it, the better."*
>
> ~ *Simon Raven*

Life Path 5: If 5 comes as a Life Path number for you, your path in life is to experience freedom through various circumstances in your life. You will be versatile, clever and creative. You are the explorer, investigator and researcher in the heart.

The element of inner liberation will be paramount to you and you will try to achieve it through variety of experiences; in terms of physical, emotional, sexual, mental, and spiritual. Restrictions and confinement wouldn't be able to stop you and you will keep on trying your best to break-free. However, you must know that to experience great freedom, some discipline too would be needed.

Once you discipline your health and finances, the physical experience of the freedom and adventure you seek will become easier. You will have the means to travel all over the world, experience the broader horizon and discover the marvels. However, if you are unable to manifest this in your life, your life itself then may turn into a melodrama. You may begin to centre yourself on creating this drama for emotional adventure.

Destiny Number 5: If your Destiny number is 5, your destiny is to bring change in effect. As a matter of fact your life will naturally show a pattern of change and your life-long aim will be to accept it in whatever way it comes. To you, it is simply a learning experience. Through this you gain the courage and willingness to let go of the used up and worn out elements of your life. Narrow-mindedness is a disappointment for you. You like to be flexible and open to new ideas and experiences.

Soul Number 5: If 5 comes up as your Soul number, freedom and variety becomes absolutely essential for your life. You feel like a prisoner if you are unable to experience new things and meet new people. Travel is something you deeply crave for as it broadens your horizons. You have a deep thirst for broad range of experiences.

Personality Number 5: If 5 comes up as your Personality number, you appear to be fun-loving, enthusiastic and charming. You show a sparkling side of yours to others; you appear o be well-groomed and well-dressed. People find you to be a great communicator and enjoy your company.

Birthday Number 5: When 5 comes up as your Birthday number, you become very quick-witted and clever. You show fast grasping powers, but can be very restless and high-strung. For this reason you may get bored easily. But, you're fun to be with.

Issues with 5: If not understood, the meaning of freedom can be devalued into self-indulgence, indiscipline and lack of focus. In the search for variety, the 5s may completely overlook what fitted them the best and find it difficult to make a commitment.

Many a times, it can be seen that the 5s could be playing a complete opposite role to what their actual character is supposed to be. Instead of being completely independent, they could be totally dependent on someone and later end up resenting that person for trapping them. Then to bring out the drama, they may turn their lives into a soap opera and create disharmonious relationships. Some 5s also end up stirring up their professional lives repeatedly in the lookout for adventure.

P 40-43 × 2³/₄

6 **Basic Meaning:** This is a number which tries to build harmony, peace and balance around it. Love, sacrifice and compassion are very important aspects of this number. It also has a strong sense of justice and is very righteous. This number also gives a keen sense of beauty, artistic abilities and a clear perception of balance and symmetry.

"Perhaps love is like a resting place
A shelter from the storm
It exists to give you comfort
It is there to keep you warm
And in those times of trouble
When you are most alone
The memory of love will bring you home..."

~ John Denver

Life Path 6: As a Life Path number, 6 puts you on a path where you have to balance your strong ideals with the practicalities of life. This number gives you a strong drive for perfectionism, but then, most people end up failing to meet your standards and you tend to reject whatever falls short of your higher vision of perfection. It is for you to remember and look at the bigger picture or you may just ruin your life getting caught up in petty details. Sometimes it is also important to ignore small mistakes.

You could also be very responsive towards the needs of your close ones. You try hard to live up to their expectations and often end up finding yourself falling short. Once again, you must remember that this is the vibration of balance hence, it is for you to accept yourself too, just the way you are.

One positive outlet for you would be finding ways to use your creative energies; you can be a natural healer, designer or interior decorator. You can also have a great taste for food. Another strong aspect of yours could be excellence in dealing with children. They could be naturally attracted to you.

Destiny Number 6: When 6 comes up as your Destiny number, home, family and relationships become your main areas of interest. You are able to mix and build sincere bonds with people. You also show a deep concern for your extended family and community. You are warm and compassionate and are always ready to sacrifice your own interests so that others can be looked after. You have strong sense of justice and are always seen to be balancing out situations of conflict.

Soul Number 6: When 6 comes up as your Soul number, you try to build a peaceful, harmonious and tranquil environment around you. Deep within you are very affectionate and empathetic towards people. To maintain equilibrium, you also exercise your delicate sense of diplomacy. Taking care of home, family and relationships is very important for you.

Personality Number 6: If 6 comes up as your Personality number, you appear to be very kind, warm and affectionate to people. You appear to be appreciative of beauty and art. You project home and family to be very important to you.

Birthday Number 6: As a Birthday number, 6 will make you very warm, caring and friendly. You would be very responsible, magnetic and lively. You will show abilities to comfort people. You will also be very good with handling children.

Issues with 6: For the 6s, no one is perfect enough. Hence, living with their strong idealism could be very difficult. There could be hundred right things that a person does, but, just one wrong move of theirs may make them totally flawed in the eyes of a 6 person. When on the positive side, the 6 people are always seen to be very warm and kind-hearted. They try to go out of their way to comfort people. However, if they hit their lower sides, they can be seen to be indulging in petty gossips about other people. It is the time when they falter in their own idealistic principles.

Also due to their high idealism, they often feel let down by most people and when that happens, they suddenly withdraw all warmth and support, becoming totally quiet and cold.

7 **Basic Meaning:** This is the number of spirituality, clairvoyance, philosophy and mysticism. It is the seeker in search of truth. This number gives strong introspective and analytical sides to a person. This produces strong need for spending time in isolation delving into the depths of mind. This number is highly observant and has great attention to details.

"You have to grow from the inside out.
None can teach you,
none can make you spiritual.
There is no other teacher but your own soul."

~ Swami Vivekananda

Life Path 7: Having 7 as a Life Path number means you are here to develop the qualities of your mind. Hence, you must allow yourself to get involved in more of mind-work than physical work. You are here to find trust in others and within your own body and soul. You must really look inside for light and when you have found it, you must share it with the world. However, that is very unlikely of you because you usually try to keep things to yourself only and keep maintaining the air of secrecy. The more people try to pry on you, the more you become emotionally distant.

A strong aspect of yours is, you will have strong clairvoyance and you must learn to trust it and use it to solve your material problems. Rather than looking towards someone else for an answer, just ask yourself, and then follow your instincts. You will be amazed by the accuracy of the first impression that you get about a person.

You could be drawn to areas which need intense research, attention to details and continuous learning and analysis. You feel very connected to nature and appreciate the simple, natural beauty associated with things. Superficialities repel you. You like the raw beauty of forests, trees, mountains, flowers, green grass, oceans and the vast sky.

Destiny Number 7: If 7 is your Destiny number, you end up having high analytical skills and a great brain for research. You can look beneath the surface and find the truth. You will be able to discover the answer to some of the greatest mysteries of life however; you yourself may remain a mystery for people, waiting to be understood. You strongly need your times of solitude so that you are able to be in tune with yourself. But once you come up with interesting finds, remember to share them with the world.

Soul Number 7: When 7 comes up as a Soul number, it makes you quiet, calm, reserved and a bit secretive. You crave to spend time alone, delving into the depths of your mind, developing your character. For this, you also wish to have peaceful surroundings so that you are able to pay attention to your intense thoughts. Noise and loud people disturb you. You feel fulfilled when you are connected to a peaceful, spiritual base which you can believe in.

Personality Number 7: When it comes up as your Personality number, you appear to be someone who needs a lot of space and privacy. You hold on to the element of mystery and secrecy revealing very little about how you really feel. This keeps people guessing what you could truly be like. But, you read them pretty well. People can also sense the element of spirituality about you.

Birthday Number 7: If 7 comes up as your Birthday number, it gives you intuitive and intellectual qualities. You need space and occasionally like to spend time by yourself. You have a reserved, calm and quiet personality and may as well be a bit secretive. You will also show good concentration level and strong attention to details.

Issues with 7: This number is all about developing trust and faith, but these two things don't come easy to it. The 7s may suffer from the fear of betrayal for which they may end up drawing emotional boundaries and become distant. They may appear to be complete loners, feeling safe in their own inner space. However, deep inside, they also crave for companionship, but are unable to express it. They don't understand the equation of intimacy because it again calls for trust, which they find difficult to give away. In the process, they remain misunderstood and misinterpreted. They may appear to trust only themselves and ignore everyone else's advice, but the truth is, they mostly look outside for truth. They seek it by reading several books or follow other people whom they consider to be experts. What they forget is to look inside for answers and trust their own abilities.

The 7s have a very active mind and continuously keep on thinking, coming up with fantastic ideas. But these brilliant ideas mostly never get expressed or exercised due to the fear of criticism that they suffer from.

8 *Basic Meaning:* This number is the karmic equalizer. It works on the principle of *karma*; which says, *as you sow, shall you reap.* Through this, 8 strikes a balance between material and spiritual planes and that is also represented by its shape; a circle on top and another at the bottom.

This number indicates focus, foresight, strength, will-power, energy, authority and hard-work. It has the ability to strongly exert its energy in the material or earthly plane for which it comes across as the true leader. However, by the end of the day, balance between spirituality and materialism also has to be achieved.

"Reach high, for stars lie hidden in you.
Dream deep, for every dream precedes the goal."

~ Rabindranath Tagore

Life Path 8: Having this as a Life Path pushes you towards establishing financial securities. Your purpose is to learn to own your power and use your influence first for yourself and then finally towards establishing higher spiritual goals. You could be working with issues related to money, power, authority and recognition in some way or the other. These issues would keep on arising for you time and again. Often people with this Life Path are seen to be late bloomers because the realization of inner power to them comes late. As they say, only when gold goes through a lot of rubbing, it is able to shine flawlessly. Similarly, people with this number go through initial phases of hardships. But, once they are able to realize and exercise their power, they reach great heights.

Many a times, the 8s are seen to be massively failing in one part of their lives, while suddenly becoming extremely successful in the other. You must remember, 8 never gives mid-way results. It is a number of extremes.

The symbol for 8 is basically the vertical orientation of the symbol of infinity (∞). This is the only number other than 0 which can be written over and over again on a piece of paper without lifting the pen. For this reason, it is considered to be representing endless cycles, just like 0. Often it is seen that the people with this Life Path, get caught up in repetitive cycles. When it is the cycle of success, they keep on succeeding over and over again. When it is the cycle of failures, they keep on repeating the same mistakes over and over again. As Albert Einstein said; *"The definition of insanity is doing the same things over and over again, but expecting different results"*.

So, in case you expect different results, change the inputs at the first place.

The most interesting thing with 8 is that this number can be flipped into a complete reversal. If it is an unfavorable cycle, you can turn it into the cycle of infinite abundance (∞) just by flipping your previous decisions.

Destiny Number 8: When 8 comes up as your Destiny number, you are destined to attain your goals through your own effort. When on the positive side, you are able to put hours of effort after your projects by showing massive energy and stamina. You are able to direct all your abilities towards achieving financial stabilities and business advancements. You are very ambitious and have a strong urge to reach the top rank. You wish to settle for nothing less. Sometimes this strong drive, energy and stamina also create brilliant sportsmen.

Soul Number 8: When your Soul number reduces to 8, it makes you very ambitious and goal-driven. Your soul feels fulfilled when you can make financial advancements in life. You like to take charge of situations and are able to tackle big projects efficiently. You have a lot of energy and are always ready to put effort in order to achieve your goals.

Personality Number 8: When this comes as your Personality number, you appear to be someone who is very focused, authoritative, strong, energetic and disciplined. You show prominent executive abilities and command leadership. You also appear to be materialistic and business-minded. You prefer to own high quality things and show a sophisticated taste.

However, you may appear a bit unapproachable and so you must work on showing some warmth.

Birthday Number 8: When this comes as your Birthday number, it gives you high stamina, hard-working attitude and a very high energy level. You have a taste for sophisticated and high quality things and wish to have a quality lifestyle. It is possible that you could be a bit accident-prone, so you have to keep a check on that and find ways to stay safe and healthy. You may as well appear to be a bit unapproachable, so you have to work on showing warmth.

Issues with 8: Most of the 8s feel a strong drive for handling business and finances, but some of them may feel a bit disappointed when they come to learn that their life purpose isactually to deal with materialism. It is important for them to understand that money and power are neither good nor evil. They are just mediums for achieving other bigger goals. If they devalue money, it wouldn't come to them. Hence, they must know that rich and powerful people are not always evil and poor and powerless are not always nice. At the same time, they must also not overvalue money and power and end up using these to bring people down. They must recognize spirituality as the higher goal and channelize their achievements in positive directions.

8 is a number of extremes. So, the 8s see the world as completely black or completely white. They are unable to see the middle shades. This also creates a problem for them when they enter into arguments. They go to any level to win the argument and

completely fail to see the other person's perspective. In the process they end up hurting people and losing friends.

9 **Basic Meaning:** This is a number of selflessness, empathy and universal love. This number is like the queen; tall, statuesque, yet concerned and deeply connected to humanity. This number gives a broader view of humanity and a sincere concern for the betterment of the masses. People with this number are very generous and they wish to make the world a better place.

> *"Our fingerprints don't fade*
> *From the lives we touch."*

> *~ Judy Blume*

Life Path 9: When 9 comes up as your Life Path number, yours is the path of universal love, peace, tolerance and compassion. This is the most evolved number in Numerology and is considered to be the strongest of all vibrations. This is why, this is the highest path of all and you are here to live with high integrity and serve as role-model for others. As a result, even when you don't try to be the centre of attention, somehow people end up putting you there anyway. You don't think you know everything, but people think that you know it all anyway. You just appear to be perfect and things simply seem to be falling in place for you as if you are blessed by divinity. People can sense a strong sense of idealism in you.

You will realize that the true way to happiness for you will come from serving others. This is why, by some way or the other, you will end up being in a path of helping and supporting people. You can be great as a doctor, therapist, counselor, teacher or a healer. Your strong artistic sense can also put you in the field of art, photography or designing.

Another interesting side of 9 is, this vibration is too connected to its past. Hence, people with this Life Path are able to maintain lifelong strong connections with their birth parents. They feel deeply responsible towards them.

This Life Path is also about a strong sense of determination to follow something one deeply believes in. This belief comes from listening to the heart. However, there still could be temptations towards following the mind. You must remember 9 is also about intuitions. It is important for you to listen to your intuitions too before making any important decisions.

Destiny Number 9: If 9 comes up as your Destiny number, your destiny then is to become the true leader of the masses; the one who leads through kindness and compassion. You will show an idealistic attitude and would wish to improve the world and make it a better place for all. Through you, many others too will have their own realizations and evolve into better human beings. You may go through many tests in life but you will come out of them unharmed.

Soul Number 9: When 9 comes up as your Soul number, you remain deeply concerned about everyone who is around you. This number gives you enormous sympathy for the masses and you are able to deeply feel their pain. You feel fulfilled when you are able to do something for their betterment in some way. You are very sensitive and loving, you need to have and give love, but your love is impersonal. It extends beyond the people in your close circle. You also feel concerned regarding unresolved family issues and feel fulfillment when you are able to resolve them.

Personality Number 9: When this comes as your Personality number, you appear to be wise, tolerant, selfless and compassionate. You lead people with your warmth and kindness and people see you as the true leader. They count on you, look up to you and come to you for advice when things go terribly wrong in their lives. You make them feel better by showing them acceptance and empathy.

Birthday Number 9: When it comes as your Birthday number, it makes you broad-minded, idealistic, helpful and compassionate. It also gives you strong artistic abilities; many great artists are born under this vibration. You will also be very socially-driven and charming; wanting to chase the bigger and more idealistic goals.

Issues with 9: Many people born under this vibration are born with physical, emotional or even mental issues. Events occur in their lives which take them upward on the path of wisdom, integrity and spirituality. They just end up teaching by example anyhow. Many 9s at the beginning of their lives may ignore their intuitions completely by following only their minds. Through life experiences they end up learning to trust their own inner voice.

Too much of idealism could also be an issue with the 9s. They expect the same amount of idealism from others as well, not realizing that by expecting others to be idealistic, they break their own idealism. It is for them to understand each one of us is born to serve a unique purpose with a unique path to follow. Others may have a different path to follow.

5.   ZERO

Before we advance to understanding what the play of multiple digits in a number code may mean, we must first understand the concept of zero. Zero has a very special importance in Numerology and nothing is more abstract than this concept.

"Black holes are where God divided by Zero."

~ Albert Einstein

Zero represents one of the greatest paradoxes of human thought. It is different from all other numbers in many ways. For instance, all other numbers can express physical quantities. They can be added and subtracted yet again to derive more complex physical quantities. On the other hand, zero represents nothing. It doesn't make a difference if you add or subtract any number with zero. So, it perhaps symbolizes something which really doesn't exist in real form. Yet, it can be achieved by subtracting two identical numbers which exist, so, we may think that zero exists too; as if acting as a balancer.

It is interesting to note when zero comes as a postfix to some number, it indicates ten times strength of the base value. (20 = 2 x 10). In the language of Numerology it can be said 0 empowers the number it follows. It is the hidden power which superficially seems to be not there, yet is there behind the scenes, enhancing and strengthening the number.

You cannot have a 0 as a base value in your Personality Chart, but you can have it in the finer double-digit codes. For instance, your Life Path/Destiny/Soul/Personality/Birthday could have a 0 in the hidden form of double-digit codes like 10/1, 20/2, or 30/3. In that way, you could be having this hidden power of 0 without having the realization of it.

This hidden power can be seen in many forms. When 0 follows 1, it gives a person the gift of unusual strength. It makes the 10/1 physically and mentally stronger than any other variety of 1. When it follows 2, it gives the gift of intense emotions and empathy. People with a 20/2 can sense the emotional ambience around them more strongly than any other variety of 2. They can be called the most intuitive variety of 2. When it follows 3, it makes the person extremely talented with speech. However, because the quality of 0 is that it cannot be seen, this immense power in a person always remains hidden unless the person learns how to manifest it. It is only around the time of maturity that a person learns to take charge of these hidden gifts and develops his complete persona. To know more about maturity, refer to **Chapter 9**.

6. THE COMPOUND NUMBERS 10-9⁰

In Chapter 4 we discussed about the single-digit or the Cardinal base values. In this Chapter we are going to see how the finer double-digit values or the Compound Numbers work. For a bird-eye view into your Numerology Chart, studying just the Cardinal Numbers would be sufficient as when you read them, you will already have the base information. This base information would always stand true. It won't get diminished when you read the meaning of the Compound Numbers on which they are based on. You must see the information provided by the Compound Numbers as additional information to the already existing information of the Cardinal base Numbers. This will enable you to find the complete picture of how exactly you must express your talents. The Compound Numbers add further to your uniqueness.

Your Uniqueness is your magic...

For instance, the Cardinal Number 4 can be based on either of the Compound Numbers 13, 22, 31 or 40 and the meaning of each Compound Number will be slightly different from the other. 4 can also be based on 58 but 58 will first reduce to 13 and then to 4. So, in that case, 58 doesn't remain the final double digit code, but is the first sum total. The more we delve deeper, more information we acquire, hence the sum total is also an important code that we can use for further clarity.

Once again, the basic meaning of the numbers wherever they appear, doesn't change, only the interpretation changes as per their placement. This is a thumb rule which you must always remember. You must also understand that the Compound Numbers are nothing but interplays of Cardinal Numbers paired together. For instance if you consider the code 62/8, you have to understand that it is basically an interaction of 2 working through 6 and finally achieving 8. Mentioned below are the brief meanings of the Compound Numbers from 10 to 99.

10 It is the number 1 born again with an empty number column, hence, it can be considered as a reincarnation of 1 with ten times the power. For this reason this version of 1, can come across as a more powerful leader. It gives strong abilities to clearly think and make decisions.

11 This is a Master Number. You can find more on Master Numbers in *Chapter 7*. This is the most intuitive of all numbers. It is also intensely emotional, but in addition to that, it also has strong leadership abilities. However, the realization of these finer abilities would only happen when you decide to look beyond the range of the base vibration 2 and rise above it. This vibration may create a leader of some sort. You will have a strong desire to uplift others which will make you a visionary.

12 It is a 2 working through a 1 and represents individuality working through togetherness, personal interests working through cooperative efforts and needs of self versus the needs of others. With this number you may appear to be easy-going from the outside but will end up showing great level of tolerance, poise and inner strength. You will come across as highly uncommon, wise, creative and innovative. We have 12 months in a year and 12 hours in half a day, hence it can also mean completion on some levels.

13 This is a very important number in Numerology and there is a great deal of misconception surrounding it. People fear this number and try to avoid it.

I'd say 13 is a very strong number and can have immense potential, but only when the meaning associated with it is understood. In Numerology it considered to be the number of change and transformation. It keeps on creating continuous renewals in life. When you have this number, it is important for you to stay humble and flexible and keep on working towards your goals. Your life will continuously present changing situations in front of you. You must have an open mind and be receptive towards new ideas.

14 This is a number which will be exposed to a variety of information and experiences. If you have this number, it is for you to keep on adapting to changing situations while maintaining a sense of purpose and discipline. Without discipline, it can lead to unhappiness. With this number, your strength and integrity will be continuously tested. This number also indicates a strong sexual side to your character

15 6 is already a very magnetic number and this compound code of 6, further enhances the charm of 6 by combining the dynamic and charismatic energies of 1 and 5 together. You are purposeful, curious, flexible and responsible. You are also loving, caring, forgiving and tolerant. You have the ability to grasp information quickly and apply it. However, you may at times become a bit self-indulgent. This number emphasizes on the material aspects of life. It shows a delicate talent towards obtaining money, support and favors. Apart from all this, there is also a need for personal space and a drive for chasing spiritual goals.

16 With this number, you are very intelligent and magnetic. The compassionate and caring qualities of the 6 playing through the dynamic and domineering qualities of 1, gives you the charm that no one can ignore. However, this may lead you towards ego-inflation and you may look down on others. It is important that you keep a check on your ego and never use your power to put people down or else, your inflated ego will be cleansed. Through the cleansing process you will be made to realize your true place in the universe. It is important that you learn the value of relationships.

17 This number indicates spiritual principle working through individualism generating tangible and material results. You would show a great brain for creative thinking, research and investigation. You will have a sharp mind and excellent concentration levels. This coupled with foresight and leadership abilities will create a strong base for fame and recognition. You must base yourself on material goals, but at the same time, you also need to be true to your spiritual and moral values. You must trust the creative, intellectual and imaginative forces within you.

18 1 and 8 both are very dynamic numbers hence this vibration gives you a lot of vitality and leadership skills. It also gives you very strong imagination and intuition. You could be a great dreamer. However, you may feel some disharmony between your logical and imaginative mind, finally allowing the brain to rule over the heart. 1 and 8 both can be very self-centered numbers. Whereas the final base value 9 is highly idealistic and intensely sensitive. So, within you, there can also be a conflict between these opposing ideologies, but ultimately tolerance and compassion will be expressed and that will enable you to heal people.

19 This number makes you very energetic and expressive. You are able to show strong leadership abilities coupled with a strong drive for power. This number is strongly connected with both; ego and humanity; selfishness and selflessness. 1 is the number of beginnings, 9 is the number of completions and the final code once again reduces to 1, hence, this can be a highly meaningful number which can indicate rebirth or reincarnation.

20 Out here the God Power 0 follows 2 hence the elements of emotion and intuition are further enhanced. Unless the hidden power of 0 is realized, it may make a person suffer from oversensitivity. But, once the power is realized and control over emotions is learnt, it gives the person the ability to sway the masses through intuitive understanding. It is possible that such a person may continuously face the challenge of having to make choices while being able to see both sides of the coin very clearly.

21 This number stands for creativity, individuality and innovation through emotional expression, balance and cooperation. This vibration is highly intuitive. It is similar to 12, but scores more on psychic abilities. People with this vibration may face initial challenges in terms of insecurity and self-doubt, but as they learn to express their intense emotional and creative energies in positive ways, they will begin to gain more confidence and see general good fortune. On the negative side, this vibration may cause tendencies towards procrastination and fear of change.

22 This is a Master Number vibration and is more commonly called the master builder. You can find more on Master Numbers in **Chapter 7**. This is the most powerful of all the master numbers and when on a positive side, it creates individuals who have vivid imaginations. They can clearly think and bring the most far-reaching dreams into reality. However, when on the negative side, they may become completely impractical and ignore the small, but important steps for creating strong foundations. This number has the potential to be the most successful of all numbers.

23 This number gives you strong communication skills. You will be clever, dynamic and quick-witted. You would seek variety in life. But, there is a possibility that you could be a late bloomer. This is because you may take some time in gaining confidence on your personal powers. Initially you could majorly be overwhelmed with acute sensitivities and self-doubt. You may also show some indiscipline, but with time, you will realize your power.

24 This vibration ensures that you are a very warm, helpful and comforting kind of a person. You are someone who loves home, children and family and wishes to build security. You are very patient, tolerant and generous. You are also very good with handling finances.

25 The number of curiosity 5, works through the number of intuition 2 and achieves the number of psychic abilities 7. This code is surely very strong on spirituality and clairvoyance. You will show excellent observation skills, great attention to details and very high concentration level. Most codes reducing to 7 create loners, but because 2 and 5 both seek to work in groups, so this would come across as one of the more sociable 7s.

26 6 works through 2 and achieves 8. All the three are practicality numbers. You will show strong business sense and foresight. You will be good with planning and managing. However, you can be a bit disorganized in your love-life. There can also be chances of getting involved in impulsive relationships. Always remember, whenever the base vibration is 8, the principle of *karma* is active. Hence, have clear intensions.

27 7 works through 2 and achieves 9. All the three are very spiritual numbers and hence, this vibration has great spiritual potential. You will show great strength of intellect. You would also show a strong potential for handling businesses. There is tremendous potential associated with this number. You can also be a great counselor, healer or even an artist.

28 8 works through 2 and reduces to 10 first and then to 1. This can be seen as a variation of 10. However, as it works through 2, as compared to a basic 10, it shows more patience and kindness. With this, you are progressive, ambitious, determined and responsible. You have a lot of vitality and are always ready for action. You are self-motivated and brave.

29 This one reduces to 11 first and then to 2, hence this can be considered as a variation of 11 which is a Master Number. You can find more on Master Numbers in *Chapter 7*. This vibration definitely makes you very unconventional, dynamic and generous. You also are very wise and have great foresight however you could be suffering from indecision. You will be somewhat in two minds, unable to decide. It is important to not lose sight of the goals.

30 With the God Power 0 behind it, this is the higher realm of 3. You have great creativity and great flair of speech. Through your words, you are able to uplift and motivate people. You also show a great sense of humor and are very optimistic and jovial. Your mind is orderly and logical for which you will also be able to handle large assignments or address to a large group of people. Your charm will attract many people towards you.

31 This is one of the most extroverted varieties of 4. With this, you become creative, fun-loving, independent, ambitious and expressive. You also show a good brain for research and always try to get into the depth of any subject that inspires you. You try your best to prove your point, at times to the extent of being quarrelsome. You have great strength and are able to stand in the face of difficulties. It is important for you to be systematic.

32 This number has a lot of curiosity and creativity. It will also make you very sensitive and intuitive and you may have emotional ups and downs. This number is very powerful. With this you can be able to attract masses. You will also show great communication skills and will be able to learn multiple languages. With this number, you must set your goals high and rely on your intuitions.

33 This once again is a Master Number and you can learn more about Master Numbers in **Chapter 7**. This is considered to be the Christ vibration because it plays the savior of the world. You will be a great teacher inspiring others to follow your path. You have a strong sense of idealism and justice and are able to show courage in difficult situations.

34 This number makes you highly intelligent and gives you massive concentration level. You will be practical and conventional, yet spiritual and philosophical as well. You would like to stick to the facts, yet you will also be very receptive towards new ideas. You will show a knack for writing.

35 This number gives you tremendous energy levels and creativity. With that, it also gives fine business sense and foresight. You have a strong and forceful personality and with that you are also expressive, social and friendly. However, you may find difficulties with working in partnerships.

36 This number gives you a very strong sense of responsibility and makes you highly dependable. At the same time, the combination of 3 and 6 reducing to 9 makes you highly creative and uncommon because all the three numbers are numbers of creativity. You will be imaginative, kind, broad-minded and generous and will find great joy in uplifting other people.

37 You are a very individualistic person. In the exterior you may appear to be calm and happy-go-lucky, but inside you have very intense feelings and imaginations. You are intellectually and philosophically sound and love to read books. However, you can be a little scattered or disorganized.

38 This reduces to 11 before the final reduction and hence creates a Master Number vibration. You can find more on Master Numbers in *Chapter 7*. You are highly spiritual and intuitive, yet you are able to balance it with your common sense and realistic attitude. You wouldn't easily admit the existence of your intuitive side. You will be successful with earning and handling money and will also be able to create harmonious environment around yourself.

39 This is 9 working through 3, which means the creativity and vibrancy of 3 is expressed, but the idea behind that would be to build a better and more functional world for the masses. You wish to inspire people in a big way however you can be highly emotional and would find it difficult to take criticism and rejection. This is also a love vibration and it makes you very romantic.

40 The God Power 0 follows the 4 and further intensifies its qualities. You are highly methodical and systematic. You like to base your work on solid strategies. You also have strong mathematical talents and a very analytical mind. You are always eager to learn more on your topic of interest. You are poised and level-headed and show remarkable emotional balance.

41 1 works through 4 and reduces to 5. This makes you highly capable of making detailed plans and also gives you the courage to take responsibility. You are also flexible and open to new ideas. You like change and adventure, but at the same time, you also try to secure your future and try to accomplish tangible results. The only negative aspect associated with this number is selfishness and that needs to be kept under check.

42 This number makes you tactful, diplomatic, friendly, cooperative and practical. You are also a good strategist and can be politically very strong. You also have a strong creative side to your brain and may work in some artistic field. You are kind and generous and have an instinctive understanding of dealing with children.

43 This number makes you very reserved, practical, dependable and composed. It also gives you a very high level of concentration and makes you more of a perfectionist. You are an optimist and you always think on constructive terms.

44 This too is a Master Number. You can read more on Master Numbers in *Chapter 7*. This number makes you extremely hard-working, practical, technically sound, disciplined and cautious. You always wish to see tangible results when you put any effort. This is an excellent business number and it gives you excellent sense of handling finances.

45 Out here, 4 and 5 are the two opposites paired together. 4 sets boundaries and secures future, while 5 wants to break them. The final base value is 9, which ends up pursuing worldly and compassionate goals. With this vibration, you could be involved in international projects however within you there could be conflicting ideas which you will struggle to balance.

46 This once again is a variation of 10. It makes you very confident and strong-willed and gives you strong leadership qualities too. However it can make you a bit unrealistic with a very strong drive for perfection. You must remind yourself to be humble and practical. When you do so, you will receive financial gains.

47 This once again is a variation of Master Number 11. You can find more on Master Numbers in *Chapter 7*. Out here the philosopher 7 works through the pragmatist 4 and achieves the intuitive 2 as the base value. Hence, this number will create a conflict between practical and intuitive sides of your mind. When you learn to achieve the balance between two sides, you will gain both financial and creative success.

48 4 and 8, both are practicality numbers. The base-value 3 is a creativity number. This number hence gives you strong sense of handling finances by not losing your creativity. You are sincere, reliable and imaginative.

49 You will have a very practical mind, yet you will also show strong sensitivity and intuition. You will have a hard-working and methodical approach and will also be level-headed, poised and patient. This would create a perfect combination for material success. However, you must maintain high principles, discipline, humility, systematic approach and honesty.

50 With the God Power 0, this is 5 intensified. You will be confident, free-spirited, versatile, adaptable, curious, intelligent and imaginative. You will be able to strike excellent conversations with people. This vibration also activates a strong need for travel and adventure.

51 This number is very similar to 15. However, out here, because 5 comes before 1, this is more independent and freedom-loving as compared to 15. In addition to that, this number makes you very righteous and ethical. You have strong principles and you stand for what you believe in. You could be placed in positions where you will have to make balanced judgments or settle disputes.

52 This vibration is very similar to 25, but is more free-spirited and broad-minded. You could be highly philosophical and spiritual. You are able to read beneath the surface and understand highly abstract concepts. You need occasional periods of solitude for introspection.

53 This number is very similar to 35, but is more energetic, active and verbal. This number makes you creative, hard-working and authoritarian. You have strong opinions and no tolerance for grays. You take action or argue for what you think is correct. Your high energy levels make you fit for sports or any other activity which requires more dynamism.

54 This is very similar to 45, but as 5 comes before 4 out here, this is less organized and more restless as compared to that. You are observant, realistic and flexible. You are also broad-minded, socially aware and generous. However, there could be a bit of impatience due to which you may find it difficult to finish your work.

55 This is yet again a Master Number. You must check *Chapter 7* for more insight on Master Numbers. With a combination of double 5s reducing to 1, this number is highly freedom-loving and individualistic. You will be highly curious and will continuously seek and retain information. You will have a way with words and will also show great flexibility and versatility. You will have strong social abilities, yet at times, you would wish to have your own space. This number may also be indicative of the birth of a new idea, or a new you.

56 This is also a Master Number as it reduces to 11 before the final reduction. See *Chapter 7* for more information on Master Numbers. In this number, 6 is working through 5, both of which represent opposite qualities. So, you could be torn between your acute sensitivities and your need for freedom. You wish to have liberty, yet seek emotional bonds. You try to be individualistic, yet end up blending with the crowd. You want to become popular and for that, you need to strike a balance. You must avoid disagreements and find the middle path.

57 This number makes you highly intelligent, creative and unusual. You will be able to understand and uplift others. You are usually optimistic, but could be prone to having swings in your mood; from very jovial to very gloomy.

58 You are adaptable and creative, yet emotionally balanced and practical. You analyze situations thoroughly before building your strategies. You don't miss out on details and your mind is continuously active. You have the flexibility to quickly realize opportunities and act upon the situation. You are not very aloof, yet you don't mind occasional times of solitude.

59 This number makes you flexible, socially aware and very eloquent. No one would be able to win an argument with you. Your mind is sharp and quick.

You can actually do multiple tasks at a time. Apart from that, you have strong opinions and have the zeal to stand by them.

60 Once again, the God Power 0 comes after the number 6 and intensifies it. You are reliable, supportive, righteous, creative, kind-hearted and confident. You also have a strong healing hand. However, sometimes the drive for perfection within you could be so strong that you would decide to settle for only the best and nothing less.

61 This number indicates independence and introspection through relationships, balance and harmony. Your need for relationships is strong, however, ultimately you chase spirituality through the understanding of your associations. You are highly intuitive and idealistic, yet pragmatic. You deeply care for others, yet you are also selfish.

62 This number is very similar to 26, but is a little less self-conscious and sensitive. You can work in groups and can manage them. You have foresight and efficiency. You will also be successful in handling finances with a strong inclination towards benefitting your family through that.

63 This number is very similar to 36, but is a little less demonstrative than that. With this, you are highly creative, compassionate, generous and dependable. You wish to make the world a better place, but wouldn't go too much out of your way to do so because you have a fine balance of emotions and logical thinking.

64 This number is very similar to 46, but a little less systematic and more creative than that as it is expressed through 6. With this, you are very charming and individualistic. You are self-sufficient and independent and are able to manage enterprises. You don't like interference from other people in your work. You are hard-working, responsible and pragmatic and you never lose your focus. You are also a good judge of human character.

65 This once again is a Master Number and you must check *Chapter 7* for more insight on Master Numbers. This number is similar to 56, but is more domestic and less fluctuating as compared to that. This number makes you patient, pragmatic and wise. You also show fine diplomacy and managerial skills. However, you must remember to always focus on the positive aspects of life.

66 This also is a Master Number vibration and for more insight on Master Numbers, you must check *Chapter 7*. This number makes you highly magnetic, intelligent, responsible and generous. You could also be strongly idealistic in your views. You are also practical and have a strong sense of handling finances. You love everything beautiful and would wish to surround yourself in beauty.

67 You are practical, analytical and systematic. You believe in harmoniously building security for the future and handle money very well. Home and family is important to you. At the same time, you are also very creative and inventive. You are able to appreciate beauty and art.

68 This is a strong business number. You have presence of mind and a way with words and can be a great negotiator. Although outwardly you may appear to be very calm and poised. But, in reality you are always able to make clever strategies to be on the right side of the table. You are broad-minded, flexible and receptive towards new ideas.

69 You are extremely creative, responsible and compassionate. You are also very generous and ready to sacrifice your own interests for others. You have the determination and energy needed for monetary success, but you don't stop at just that. You then use your success for the betterment of the society.

70 This is 7 intensified with the God Power 0. You are basically a loner, but can also be surprisingly good in relationships because you are able to understand people well and are a good judge of character. The 0 out here acts as a protection. You are intelligent, practical, thoughtful, as well as highly intuitive, spiritual and philosophical. You seek the truth and are ready to probe into the depths for it.

71 With this number, you will be able to master a skill which you'd focus your energies on. You will not be distracted by external sources and will strongly maintain your center. You are hard-working, focused, determined and disciplined. However at times you need to take life on a less serious note and loosen up a bit.

72 You are highly spiritual, intuitive, generous and compassionate. You are able to work in partnerships for a bigger cause. You are practical, broad-minded and ambitious. You enjoy solving problems for the welfare of the masses. You are also very cautious with your resources and can be very selective about the goals and the people that you choose.

73 It is a variation of 10 and also very similar to 37. You are determined, self-sufficient and introspective. You are comfortable even when you are alone and pursuing your own purpose. You also have great creative power inside you.

74 This once again is a variation of Master Number 11 and you can find more on Master Numbers in **Chapter 7**. With this number, you are highly intuitive and spiritual. However, there is also a practical side to you. You have high concentration levels and you like to continuously seek more and more knowledge. Relationships are also important to you. You are poised, supportive and cooperative and are willing to contribute in team efforts.

75 This number is very similar to 57, but is more introspective as compared to that. You are highly intelligent, imaginative, optimistic and spiritual. You value your personal space and freedom. You have high ambitions and a potential for many achievements, but that would need steady effort from your part.

76 You are introspective, spiritual, pragmatic, reliable and responsible. You are a good planner and organizer and you tend to make your decisions based on logic and common sense rather than emotions. You have a clear mind and can be highly skilled in your trade. You have the power to translate any idea into reality.

77 This is a Master Number vibration and you can find more on Master Numbers in *Chapter 7*. With this number, you are highly intuitive, spiritual, inventive and intelligent. You are able to read and understand others. No detail can be hidden from your eyes. You are also highly magnetic and can strongly draw people towards yourself. You are flexible, clever and cautious.

78 7 stands for the spiritual realm and 8 for the material. With the combination of the two, you are ready for accomplishments in both. You will be blessed with affluence and luxury and a life of fulfillment. You understand that it takes a systematic lifestyle to maintain a balance. With the material side of life taken care of, you will be able to focus your energies on spiritual aspects.

79 You are intuitive and introspective. You wish for the betterment of humanity through spiritual understanding of life. You prefer literary and scientific activities that can support a bigger cause. You have a broad-minded approach towards life and do not indulge in petty gossips.

80 Out here 8 is followed by the God Power 0. With this number, you will have great foresight. You will be able to see the bigger picture and have a broader perspective. It is a terrific business number and symbolizes power, strength, energy and control and all these aspects must be used for the highest good of the mankind. It also represents the principle of karma magnified. Hence, you have to be clear with your intensions.

81 This number is very similar to 18, but out here, as 1 works through 8, and creates a more materialistic approach as compared to 18. You are business-minded, yet you also have somewhat of an idealistic outlook and tolerance for diverse belief systems. You are highly focused and self-sufficient. You can be spiritual too, but often your spirituality is over-shadowed by materialism. The negative side is; it can be sometimes very ruthless and violent.

82 This number is basically 28 reversed, hence very similar to it, but a bit different. As compared to 28, it is more domineering and competitive. With this, you are self-reliant, pragmatic, strong, courageous and energetic. You have a materialistic drive and are very individualistic, yet you also value cooperative efforts and team-work. This duality of wanting to collaborate, yet remaining unfettered, may cause lack of durability in marriage.

83 This is 38 reversed and hence similar to that. As compared to 38, this has a stronger materialistic drive. Like 38, this also is a variation of Master Number 11 and you can find more on Master Numbers in **Chapter 7**. With this number, you are able to strike the fine balance of common sense and intuition. Rather, it can be said that intuition takes a backseat. You have a logical and practical attitude and are good with handling business and finances.

84 This is 48 reversed and is very similar to that. As compared to 48, it has more foresight and bigger imaginations and can be a little less organized. With this, you are very hard-working and purposeful. You are also very imaginative. The combination of 8 and 4 creates an energy which makes you deal with tangible products which you could be creating with your hands. There is some insecurity associated with this number for which you may face some initial struggles in life.

85 This is the reverse of 58 and is very similar to that. As compared to 58, it is less impulsive and flexible and has more foresight and organizational skills. This number makes you clever, curious, domineering, focused and energetic. You are quick to realize opportunities and act upon them. You have a very business-minded approach towards life.

86 This is the reverse of 68 and is in many ways similar to it, but is more ego-centric as compared to that. With this number, your overall outlook towards life is adventurous, yet somewhere down the line you are also highly practical. The conflict between personal freedom and commitment is always a pressing issue in your mind.

87 This is the reverse of 78 and in many ways similar to it. This has combined energies of 8 and 7 reducing to 6. With this number you have a practical mind, yet there is also an intense spirituality within you. You are good with handling finances. You are also highly responsible and protective about your immediate family or community.

88 This is a Master Number vibration and you can find more on Master Numbers in *Chapter 7*. This number has double 8s reducing to 7, hence, it is full of contradictions. There is a constant conflict between materialism and spirituality. However, this can be a very powerful business number and is usually seen to be good with money. With this number, you are apt with handling finances. You have a highly practical and scientific approach, yet, you also show a fine sense of spirituality. However, you may find difficulties in maintaining interpersonal relationships.

89 In this number, philantropy is working through materialism. This number gives you a fine sense of handling business and finances and with that an idealistic view of the world. You focus on higher goals and wish to make the world a better place. You like to be socially active and dislike being left alone. This number may bring many tests, but you will have the power to overcome all obstacles.

90 Out here, 9 is followed by the God-Power 0. This number makes you a complete humanitarian. You are highly idealistic and have great compassion for mankind. You are generous and inspiring. You have a sophisticated nature. You remain aloof, but are respected by people around you.

91 You are compassionate and independent. You also are highly energetic and determined towards achieving your goals. You will have strong opinions and idealism. Chances are you will be highly successful in any creative field, but you may find it difficult to keep money.

92 This number reduces to Master Number 11 before the final reduction and can be considered to be a variation of 11. You can find more on Master Numbers in *Chapter 7*. With this number, you are highly intuitive, spiritual, kind and compassionate. You are also tolerant and cooperative. You have a broad view of the world, yet interpersonal relationships are also highly important to you.

93 With this number, you are highly creative and also concerned about social causes. You wish to express your creativity by improving your surroundings, hence you could be interested in architecture and landscaping. You wish to combine imagination with drama and bring a positive message to the world. You have an upbeat energy and are highly social as well.

94 You are realistic and pragmatic and through your practical approach, you wish to make a difference to the world. You are focused and have a methodical approach, but you may lack flexibility. You find it difficult to adjust to changes of any kind and are very attached to old habits.

95 You are broad-minded, curious and have a sharp mind. You are able to quickly grasp everything and have a wide variety of interests. However, you quickly tend to lose interest also. You are very social and flexible. You have a strong desire for travel and adventure and may become a bit impractical in the lookout for new experiences.

96 This is the reverse of 69 and in many ways similar to that. With this, you are compassionate, self-sacrificing and warm. You are deeply concerned about the welfare of your home and family. You are also highly responsible and idealistic.

97 In this number, introspection works through tolerance. You have a sensitive, intuitive, spiritual and analytical mind. You have a deep desire to accumulate knowledge and wisdom in any form. You prefer scientific, metaphysical or literary subjects which can create more awareness in the world.

98 This is a practical number with humanitarian goals. On one hand you have a strong knack for dealing in business and finances. On the other hand, you also have strong tolerance and compassion for the mankind. For this reason, people may find it difficult to understand you fully. They may not understand whether you are driven by selfishness or you are actually selfless.

99 This is a Master Number variation of the base value 9 and out here the number 9 is further raised in its perfection. You can find more on Master Numbers in *Chapter 7*. With this number, you are broad-minded, tolerant, compassionate and highly idealistic. You are also self-sufficient and self-sacrificing. You are highly graceful and sophisticated.

7. THE MASTER NUMBERS

Now that you know how exactly to work with Compound Numbers, it will be easier for you to understand the concept of Master Numbers. In Numerology every number is considered to be equally special and no number is either superior or inferior to any other number. All is one.

The final Cardinal base values are always more important than the finer double/triple-digit Compound codes and this is a thumb rule. However, there are some exceptions one of which is the case of Master Numbers.

You must first know that every Master Number is basically a Compound Number first. But, the Master Numbers stand out because they have repeats of the same digit unlike the other general Compound Numbers where each digit varies. It is a thumb rule; every time a number repeats, its strength increases. Whether it repeats in your blueprint, or within a specific code that you're dealing with, you cannot ignore the significance or the strength of the repeating value. It will show its effect surely.

So, in a Master Number, the repeating number is equally strong as the final Cardinal base number. This means the interpretation of these numbers needs some special attention because of the strong duality associated with them. It is always seen that Master Numbers always have profoundly powerful meanings and are considered to be having more potential than the other numbers. However, unless the potential is tapped, it doesn't count.

Open your heart and your mind
to the world of possibilities...
In the life through which you travel,
you can go on rediscovering ourselves...

Tapping the potential of the Master Numbers needs a certain level of maturity which is only achieved with time and experience. Unless the realization of personal powers or maturity is achieved, the Master Number only produces restlessness due to the duality associated with it. Once a person learns to tame the wild power of the Master Numbers, there can be immense possibilities for growth. *Refer to Chapter 9 on Maturity Numbers.*

It is a popular notion that there are only three Master Numbers; 11, 22 and 33. When I began my study on the subject, I too believed the same. But then, I realized perhaps something was not complete. 11, 22 and 33 were higher octaves of 2, 4 and 6 and that didn't complete the full sequence of base values from 1 to 9. What about the other cardinal numbers? Why wouldn't they have their higher octaves too? I slowly realized the power of the other repeating numbers too and understood that each base value from 1 to 9 must have a Master Number associated with it. Mentioned below are the specific dualities associated with each

Master Number. When you read, you will be able to realize what exactly makes these numbers so special. Why they are so much more than their base values.

11/2

Master Number 11 accentuates the base vibration 2 and has all the aspects associated with 2. It is highly intuitive, compassionate and cooperative. But, that's not all. Out here the qualities of 2 becomes further charged with the qualities of the repeating 1s.

1 is about leadership, dynamism, individualism, independence and innovation. 1 is active while 2 is passive. Hence this number is full of contradictions and dualities. It flickers between greatness and self-sabotage. The leadership abilities, foresight and innovation can only be expressed when the finer meanings are realized and focus is found. If the higher meanings remain untapped, it will play the role of the base-vibration 2.

22/4

Master Number 22 accentuates the base vibration 4. The number 4 is called the builder and hence 22 represents the Master Builder. It has all the aspects of 4 and much more than that. 4 is associated with problem solving, material achievements, hard-work and practicality. While on the other hand, 2 carries the qualities of sensitivity, intuition and vivid imagination. For this reason, 22 represents imagination, dreaming and building the dreams in broad terms. With this number it is important to see that you maintains a practical and step-by-step approach or else you wouldn't be able to sustain your grand imaginations.

33/6 This is the higher octave of the base vibration 6 and is called the Master Teacher. Out here, 3 stands for creativity and imagination, while 6 stands for community love and idealism. Hence this number is about inspiring creativity in others as well as within oneself. With this number, you will only find fulfilment when you get completely immersed in some project and are fully able to express your creative energy through it. Once you are able to find creative fulfilment, you would try to further extend it though universal sympathy, balance and idealism. You could be very high-strung and may have high standards of perfection. You may also tend to be very selfless and self-sacrificing and believe in living for a higher cause.

44/8 This is a Master Number where the base value 8 is amplified with the appearance of double 4s. Possibility of finding this Master Number is more rare as compared to 11, 22, or 33. 4 out here stands for stability, caution, method and constancy, while 8 stands for strength, foresight, determination and business sense. The good part is, out here both 4 and 8 are practically driven numbers. Hence this would have less contradiction. This number will show huge potential and would be more balanced, disciplined and steady as compared to any other variation of 8.

With this number you would plan your actions well in advance. Everything that you would do would be well-thought of. You would be rock-steady under any circumstances and face adversities with continued effort.

55/1 Master Number 55 accentuates the base vibration 1. Out here 1 stands for innovation, determination, leadership and individuality. While the repeating 5 stands for curiosity, flexibility, adventure and communication. Hence with this number you would be involved in finding the truth and sharing it with others when the truth is finally uncovered. You would be highly self-sufficient and also receptive towards new ideas. You will always be ready to experiment. You will also be very direct and spontaneous with your expressions and communication. These qualities would make you a great detective or a researcher.

66/3 This is the higher octave of the base vibration 3. Out here 6 stands for community love, responsibility and idealism, while 3 stands for communication, optimism and creativity. Hence, with this number you would be highly optimistic as well as idealistic. You would also have deep concerns for your immediate environment and community. You would try to make sure that peace, harmony, creativity, beauty and balance are always restored. You would also be highly righteous and would try to make balanced judgments. Interior decorators, artists, designers, doctors, judges or any of the people who deeply care for maintaining justice and balance in their environment, fall under this number.

77/5 This is the higher octave of the vibration 5. The repeating 7 stands for introspection, spirituality and silence, while the base value 5 stands for adventure, experiences and free-spirited energy. This vibration represents a mind which would never cease to work. With this number you would also be highly sensual and would appreciate experiences of all kind; physical or mental. You would have a great mind and terrific observation skills through which you would be able to benefit the world in many ways. Spiritual leaders, inventors, mystics, and researchers would fall under this vibration.

88/7 Master Number 88 is the higher octave of the base-value 7. If you look at the shape of the two 8s, you'll notice that they are basically 0s repeating themselves 4 times. Hence this number, in spite of being a 7 base vibration, contains infinite energy, drive and power of the four 0s. Athletes, bankers, corporate executives and business-men may all fall under this vibration. This will be all about immense physical strength and foresight teamed with a spiritual bent of mind.

Like all the other Master Numbers, this too has its own contradictions. It is intuitive and analytical, yet practical and efficient. It has a scientific and practical approach, yet is also comfortable with spiritual matters.

99/9 This is the higher octave of the already highest vibration 9. This can be seen as the teacher behind the Master Teacher. This vibration always brings with it some mammoth responsibility of taking the whole world to a higher realm. It resonates with divine consciousness. Great spiritual gurus and holy avatars fall under this vibration. They inspire masses with their compassion and undying concern for the mankind. With this number, you will be a real humanitarian and there shall be no one like you. This number demands great sacrifices. With this it is important to maintain a continuum.

8. THE MODIFIED NAME

There is hardly any woman in this world who can say that she has not faced any hair problems. Most of us aren't happy with the way our hair looks. We struggle with frizz, dryness, thinness, coarseness, lack of bounce and so many other hair issues. But the good thing is, there is always hope. So what if we don't totally like what we were born with, we can always style our hair and make it appear a bit different from how it originally was. We can groom ourselves and choose to look a little different.

When we style our hair, it acquires certain new and desirable qualities like for example shine, straightness and bounce, while the undesirable qualities like frizz or dryness are subdued. We end up looking more attractive and start emitting a whole new vibe. People sense this new spark about us, they see our hair for what it looks like from outside and begin to perceive us a little differently as compared to before. Also in our minds we begin to perceive our own image much differently. We feel happy about how our hair looks and makes us feel and this instills more confidence in our personality.

You must be wondering why I am talking about hair styling right now!

Well, a modified name is just like styling your hair!

The Modified Name creates a different perception of yours in people's minds as well as in your own mind and by doing so it creates a difference in your experience of everyday life. Ideally if it is a well-suited name, it is supposed to add some desirable qualities that were missing in your original name while subdue or balance some undesirable qualities which were present in excess. However, just the way styling wouldn't be able to change the original structure of the hair and the actual qualities would surely come out at some point, similarly Modified Name will not be able to completely change your Destiny or the qualities ingrained within you through your birth name. All that it can do is even out your day-to-day experiences and thus creating more contentment and happiness.

It is very important that the hair-style we choose complements our existing personality and doesn't go against it. Similarly, the new name that we choose should complement our existing base qualities and further enhance them but not go against them.

The new style or the new name shouldn't be chosen on impulse.

It is to be seen that through the new name choice more balance is achieved.

Many a times we may come across lopsided personalities where we may see excessive strength and determination while there may be a complete lack of tact and diplomacy. Or there could be too much of active emotions and sensitivity but a complete lack of level-headed qualities. It is then that we can choose to balance out the qualities that are present in excess with other qualities which would make the personality better-rounded. We need little bit of all qualities to create a balanced character as in our lives we will be faced with all kinds of situations and from time to time we would need to show everything; focus, discipline, energy, will-power, tact, practicality, kindness, creativity, compassion and what not. So, this means that our name should have a little bit of all numbers present in the form of letters. As we know each letter has a numeric value associated with it hence we must see that our name has a good variety of numeric values thus enabling us with qualities to deal with almost all kinds of situations because if there is a missing value, it would mean a missing quality. Also the final modified Soul, Personality and Name numbers should also be in tune with our original Personality Chart numbers.

We must value our uniqueness or the magic will be lost !

The three components of our Modified Name which are Modified Soul, Modified Personality and Modified Name are all calculated in the same way as the Soul, Personality and Destiny numbers as discussed earlier. It is to be noted that each new name that we choose, would set us in a new direction in life which would be indicated by the numbers associated with that name. When you'd study the meanings of these numbers you'd know which direction the name will slowly take you towards.

Every new number you associate with
Will have a new story to tell...

The Modified Soul number would sub-due the qualities present in your original Soul number, and add some new qualities. The Modified Personality number would sub-due the qualities present in the original Personality number and add new qualities. Likewise the Modified Name number too would sub-due the qualities present in your Destiny number and add new qualities. But, none of the core qualities would be totally lost. Your original numbers would show their effect at some point for sure.

No one can change your Destiny
If it were to change,
it won't be Destiny any more...
All that you can do is
enjoy the journey because after all,
life is actually not about the destination!

The effects of a name change would happen more quickly if the name is changed at an early age. With age, our core qualities become more solidified and hard-grained, hence at a matured age, if the name is changed, it would take some time to show results as the qualities of the new name would only assimilate into your existing personality with time. The sooner you are able to associate with and accept the new name internally, the faster would be the effect of the name. Hence, when the name change is more organic, i.e. when it is connected to your personal history in some way, it is seen to be assimilating with you quicker.

> ## *No one else but only you would know which name choice connects with you immediately and which doesn't.*

If a name doesn't feel right to you or doesn't convey what you wish to say, it is surely not the name for you. Every choice you make would have a consequence hence you must never allow anyone else to make this choice for you because it is you who will face the outcome and not them. You must also realize that there is no perfect number. Each number is equally flawed and has both positive and negative qualities associated with it. Similarly, there is no perfect name and each name would have pros and cons associated with it. It is for you to analyze all possibilities and then decide upon which direction you would like to set for your life. You must make sure that your choice is in alignment with your journey and your purpose.

P99 - 11 × 12

Lost in the Woods

Once upon a time six friends got lost in the woods. As they walked, it was difficult to know which direction they were going. Faced with uncertainties, they decided to put heads together. But each one ended up having a different opinion. One of them said, "Let's go left! My intuition tells me we must go that way. I am sure it is the way we must take" But, the second friend immediately disagreed and said, "There is no reason why we should go left! Left doesn't sound right. I think right is the right way as it sounds like rightness. I am so positive, so, let's go right"

To this, the third friend disagreed. He said, "I think it was a bad idea to come into the woods at the first place. We will be safest if we venture no further into it and try to go back where we came from. I don't get a good feeling about either left or right, I'd rather identify the patterns and find my way back home" The fourth friend immediately contradicted by saying,

"Looking back is not an option ever. We must only look forward and go forward. If we aren't able to discover new things, what then remains the meaning of life? "

The fifth friend thought he was highly clever. He said, "You're all wrong. Where is logic in your plans? I have the best strategy. Give me some time and wait till I tell you what exactly to do!" He looked here and there and soon spotted the tallest tree around. He decided to climb on it and reach the tree top and see how far the forest went. The sixth friend didn't contradict anyone, but agreed to wait for the fifth to come up with his idea.

While the fifth friend was attempting to climb to the tree top, all his other friends barring the sixth one, became impatient and went on in their own directions. While, from atop he saw the beautiful forest looming far and wide. He clearly also saw all the routes that could take them out of the woods safely. Finally he found the shortest way which would get him out faster. He immediately knew he had found the best solution and hurried down the tree to share his excitement with others. But, when he reached the ground he saw only one of them was there. All his other friends had long left. At this he was outraged and disappointed because he knew he had the best plan, yet others didn't wait to acknowledge. They were so stubborn that they just won't listen! He said to himself the others were fools as they will never find their way out and suffer as they didn't have the patience to listen to his brilliant plan. After all he was the best strategist and the wisest of them all! The sixth friend agreed to him and followed him. Both of them were soon out of the forest...

But before we conclude that this fifth friend was actually the wisest of them all, first let us look at the experiences the other four friends had:

The friend who went left by following his intuitions, soon found himself going further into the dense forest. There the trees were ancient and timeless as they disappeared into the sky. They were rough with age, yet their roughness had been worn down by the soft greenness of moss that had slowly made them home. Gnarled roots dipped into the ground and twisted branches reached down. For many days he tried, yet was unable to find his way out. He thought how foolish he was for having followed his intuitions as they didn't guide him out! He had no choice and made himself a home in the tree canopies. For his survival, he had to fight, so he learnt to make fire by rubbing stones. He also learnt to forage into the forest further, used his intuitions to find his meals. He soon realized his destiny was not to get out of the forest, but remain there. To him the forest was no more an alien land, rather it was his home and he was in perfect sync with it. He became a part of the forest and whenever any passersby were lost, he taught them survival skills that he had learnt for himself.

The friend who went right believed in living for the moment and not thinking too much about the future. He was optimistic and cheerful and decided to follow the stars. For some time he wandered in the forest cheerfully as he felt it was something exciting that he had never done before. He knew nothing can ever go wrong. Unable to foresee the possible danger, to his shock he had an encounter with looters. They took everything away from him and then forced him to play ally with them. Yet his optimism was not lost. He knew in the end, everything would be alright and nothing changed his belief. So, he remained with them as their friend with the hope that one day they will change. Little by little he made them realise how wonderful it was to bring light to people's lives and how far they had fallen in darkness. The looters slowly realized the power of positivity. The darkness within them faded as they realised from within the importance of humanity and compassion. Soon the looters too were converted into light-workers like him. Together with his new found followers this friend went on extending the domain of his optimism further to the world.

The friend, who had decided to go back, had felt it was like a trauma to venture into unknown territories of the forest. He realized he would be most comfortable at his own home. His real treasure was there and not outside. For that is where his heart belonged. What was the whole point of delving into uncertainties then! So he found his way back and stayed at home. He ventured no further than that. He strengthened his bonds with his family and community and from his home he started his own successful venture. He created a stable life for himself as well as for his loved ones. Other than that, he also knew the route to the forest. He could never forget he was once lost and decided that no one he cared for should ever go through the same trauma like he did. So he made a secure pathway through the un-trodden route. He covered its surface with loose gravel and lined it with hedges. Like a black ribbon, it disappeared into the forest. His little cosy pathway soon became a popular road lined with bright lights through which many people walked without the fear of getting lost.

The friend who decided to go straight was always known for his courage and bravery. He was a pioneer striking out alone. He went on and on under the sunless sky, through the fallen timber and thickets of weeds. The forest to him looked pure and clean as if never disturbed by any other man. He took all the routes less travelled and explored beyond the horizons. He saw the birth of communities of many beautiful saplings and visited many exotic places no one had ever been before. He discovered new dimensions and new colours. He saw wonderful new plants and animals and discovered many new tribes and traditions. There were times when he landed up in troubles, yet he was brave, clever and flexible to manoeuvre himself around them. He realized that he had the gift of free-spirit and his mind was further broadened by his experiences. He was now sure that he had chosen the best path and he was to never let it go.

The friend who waited for the fifth friend and decided to follow him was a follower in the true sense. He knew his power was in playing the support. So, he supported his chosen leader *through thick and thins and made his way out together with him. He assisted his leader with his plans and together they built a strong foundation that lasted. He was patient and considerate and was always there to listen and encourage. He played the power behind the scene and together they achieved great prosperity, success and abundance.*

***Every road led to Rome
and all reached their destinations,
yet each one had their own realization
and ended up with their own story to tell...***

Neither of the stories are right nor wrong, they are just different stories; each one equally exciting.

There can be many answers to the same question and many solutions to the same problem, yet all answers and all solutions could be correct. It didn't matter if the friends were lost together, but it was for them to decide on their path by their own. The gift of Maturity gives us the realization through which we instinctively know which path is for us to follow. We no longer waste our time trying to delve into other paths thinking it could be our way.

Just as unique as we are, each one of us is blessed with a unique Maturity Number of our own. The Maturity Number is basically the culmination of all the other five Primary Numbers in our blue-print. It can also be said it is the culmination of all our talents. All that we have inside, is there for a reason and one day, all the dots really join.

The Maturity Number is known to show the most profound effect at around the age of about 27 to 35 years, depending on our Life Path numbers. Deriving this number is very simple we just have to add our Life Path number with our Destiny number and finally reduce the value to a single digit.

For example, if the Life Path number is 21/3 and the Destiny number is 56/11/2, the Maturity Number will be 21 + 56 = 77/5.

To find the exact point of Maturity, you have to subtract your Life Path base value from four cycles of 9 (4 x 9 = 36). Hence, if your Life Path is 21/3, you can derive the point of maturity by subtracting 3 from 36 (36 – 3 = 33). So, the point of maturity in this case would be around 33 years of age.

As per Astrology the time span of around 27 years also corresponds to the first complete return of Saturn in our natal chart. The planet Saturn in astrology is called the great teacher. It takes away many wonderful things from us and makes us face challenges. It is through these challenges that we discover our true strength.

During the time span of about 27 years, Saturn visits all the planets in our chart and leads them to solidification. This in turn solidifies our personality and strengthens our mind.

However, achieving maturity is not an easy process. It comes when we face uncertainties and come up with our own unique survival strategies. The soul then truly comes in contact with the body and we are able to realize our true calling.

"What you get by achieving your goals
is not as important as
What you become by achieving your goals."

~ Henry David Thoreau

Mentioned below are descriptions of the Maturity Number base values from 1 to 9. In case you wish to find further enlightenment through the study of the unique double-digit code that you have derived, you may refer back to the brief meanings of Compound Numbers provided in **Chapter 6** and meanings of Master Numbers provided in **Chapter 7**.

_Maturity 1__:_ With this number, around the point of maturity, you feel the strong urge to find your own individuality. You are called upon to take charge and initiative as there remains no other way. You are not any more allowed to remain dependant, rather are made to fight harder and become more driven and to find your own way out. You come out as someone who is truly original and creative. You emerge as the leader and the pioneer.

Maturity 2: With this number, around the point of maturity, you realize your talent towards working in coordination with others. You begin understanding people and their motives and are also able to influence them through your persistent tactful and diplomatic ways. These talents make you highly clever and give you the ability to control people emotionally. You are also able to develop business sense by cooperating with others.

Maturity 3: With this number, around the point of maturity, you face situations which challenge your optimism. You discover ways to remain positive in the direst of circumstances. You become more fluent with your words and expression and learn to express yourself originally and creatively. Through that you are able to inspire many others and show them light. Due to your upbeat energy and positivity, you end up gaining many followers and your popularity rises.

Maturity 4: With this number, around the point of maturity, you discover your talent of finding interesting solutions to the most persistent problems. You become increasingly practical, build strong strategies and plan your moves well in advance. You become highly goal driven and develop strong methods and systems that help you in giving tangible shape to your ideas. Through your talents you are able to develop strong foundations for any organisation.

Maturity 5: With this number, around the point of maturity, you are being challenged to show adaptability in the face of uncertainty. You begin to realize how important it is to embrace change and adventure. You begin to realize the value of freedom and then there is no slowing you down any further. Your ability with words and expression grows and so does the domain of your influence. You become interested in subjects you never considered before and discover places no one has ever been before.

Maturity 6: With this number, around the point of maturity, you realize the value of your strong home base. You become concerned about the welfare of your family and your community and feel motivated to nurture and protect them. You become more responsible and dutiful than before and become involved in improving the living standards for your community. This also brings along with it a very strong business sense and the ability to efficiently deal with your resources.

Maturity 7: With this number, around the point of maturity, you realize the need to delve into the depths of your own mind further. You realize your own mind is the forest in itself and there are many mysteries in there waiting to be solved. Through this you also realize that each person other than you also holds a unique forest of their own inside their mind. You are able to read between the lines and see beneath their masks. You begin to feel fascinated when you are able to predict some of their mysteries too.

Maturity 8: With this number, around the point of maturity, you realize the value of money, stability and all earthly things. You are able to find your focus and your commitment to your goal deepens. You end up attracting situations that demand strong strategies, organisational skills and managerial abilities. With this you grow in authority and power and find financial rewards. Your foresight and common sense get noticed by many and they desire to join you in your path supporting you to achieve your goals.

Maturity 9: With this number, around the point of maturity, you realize that your life is perhaps not yours alone to enjoy. There are bigger causes to be addressed. You begin to become increasingly concerned about the well-being of the entire humanity as a whole and set yourself on a path to make the world a better place. You also begin to appreciate the beauty that surrounds you. You feel for it and wish to improvise upon that too. Through your efforts you wish to create things of lasting value from which the whole world would be able to benefit.

Once you have decoded your Personality Chart numbers, you also have to realize that you are not to allow these numbers to control you rather you must take charge of them and make them play to your advantage. It is for you to decide that you remain at the positive end of each vibration that you are born with. You are born with incredible power and potential. Each number in your chart is capable of activating an array of possibilities. The choice of what you choose to respond to, will always be yours. Your mind is a tool for you to use any way you wish. The way you use it right now, is your present pattern and at any point of time, old patterns can be broken and new ones created.

Everything is a microcosm of the macrocosm.

A cell is a single self-sustaining unit of a bigger self-sustaining unit; human body. We as independent identities are together a part of a single unit called Earth. The Earth in turn is a part of a bigger unit called the universe. The patterns are same in all levels of the cosmos and all is one. The universe is a part of "All that Is", which we may call God. Everything is really alive as all life is made from the same substance; star-dust. When you begin to see yourself enough as one, yet also a part of this collective consciousness and begin to align yourself with it, you'd be able to achieve great degrees of fulfilment.

Printed in Great Britain
by Amazon

82815313R00068